The   Snailbeach   District   Railways

£6.95

THE SNAILBEACH DISTRICT RAILWAYS – *No. 2 leaving Pontesbury Sidings on June 11th 1943.* *(L.W. Perkins)*

The Snailbeach District Railways

Eric S Tonks M.Sc., A.R.I.C.

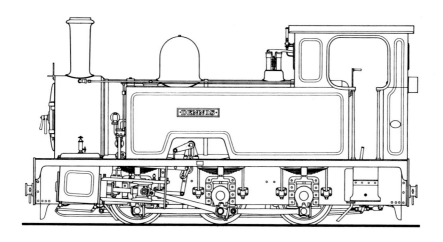

DENNIS — *Drawing by Roger West.*

The Industrial Railway Society

First published by the author in 1950
Revised and enlarged edition published by the IRS in 1974
1974 edition reprinted in 2007, second reprint 2008 ©

Published by   Industrial Railway Society
                24 Dulverton Road,
                Melton Mowbray,
                Leicestershire,
                LE13 OSF
Email   sales@irsociety.co.uk
Web site   www.irsociety.co.uk
For details of Society membership send sae to:
                Mr. B. Mettam, 27 Glenfield Crescent, Newbold, Chesterfield, S41 8SF

ISBN 978 1 901556 49 0

NOTES TO THE 2007 REPRINT
The Society is pleased to reproduce in full the definitive 1974 edition of this book by Eric S. Tonks, the late President of the Industrial Railway Society with the only changes being those noted on this page and new designs for the covers.

Following publication of the 1974 edition there have been four articles on this subject published in the Industrial Railway Society's magazine, the Industrial Railway Record, as follows:
    'More About Snailbeach' by Rodney Weaver (Issue No.70, April 1977)
    'Pontesbury Junction' by Andy Cuckson (Issue No.144, March 1996)
    'DENNIS at Snailbeach' by Allan C. Baker (Issue No.164, March 2001)
    'FERNHILL – The Snailbeach Barclay' by Andy Cuckson (Issue No.164, March 2001)

These mainly amplify the information given in Eric Tonks' book, although a few minor errors have been identified and these are listed below:

The suggestion that Driver/Fitter Gatford worked the line single-handed in the 1930s is not correct, because "Junction Man W. Jones" acted as manager ordering spares and controlling the petty cash.

The early career of No.2 locomotive (Kerr, Stuart 802) is not given, whereas we now know that it was used by Henry Lovatt & Co on the construction of the Leek & Manifold Railway before being purchased by the Admiralty at the outbreak of World War 1. After use at Ridham Depot, it was sold to Snailbeach District Railways in December 1922 via the Stoke on Trent dealer, E.C. Cornforth, and delivered to Snailbeach in March 1923.

According to Allan C. Baker quoting Colonel Stephens' records, the two Baldwin locomotives were purchased in January 1923 from Messrs Learoyd & Son of Clapton, London and sent to Snailbeach in April 1923.

Baldwin locomotive No.4 was maker's number 44522, not 44572.

Produced by Print-Rite, Witney, Oxfordshire. 01993 881662

CONTENTS

ACKNOWLEDGEMENTS

This revised edition of the booklet published in 1950 brings the story to its anticipated conclusion, and includes some fresh material that has recently come to light. For most of this I am indebted to Miss Mary C. Hill, County Archivist of Salop, who provided so much information for the original edition. My sincere thanks are also due to the Birmingham Public Libraries; Mr.C.L. Hewitt, Secretary of the S.D.R. ; Messrs Longueville & Co., Oswestry; the Executors of the late Major Dyke Dennis; the Surveyor, County of Salop; Messrs Haywards Quarries Ltd; Messrs W.G. Bagnall Ltd; the Editor of the *Shrewsbury Chronicle;* Fitter-Driver Gatford; and Messrs N.J. Allcock, R.A. Bowen, V.J. Bradley, J.L. Brown, D. Clayton, I.G.T. Duncan, A.L.F. Fuller, H. Gray, E.C. Griffith, E.J. Lees, L.W. Perkins, M. Rhodes, W.K. Williams; and to data published in *The Locomotive, The Railway Magazine, The Railway Observer* and *The Journal of the Stephenson Locomotive Society.*

There are, inevitably, gaps in the story, which further research may fill. I would be very pleased to hear from members or others who have comments to make, or extra information to offer, which can be inserted in a forthcoming issue of the "Industrial Railway Record".

ERIC S. TONKS

87 Sunnymead Road
Birmingham
February 1974

PROMOTION OF THE RAILWAY

Set in a county justly proud of the fairness of its green and smiling countryside, the Shropshire hills have for centuries been the goal of those seeking after natural beauty, to whom they offer a wonderful variety — the Wrekin, a stump of volcanic ash furred with trees from foot to summit, splendid in its majestic isolation on the Severn plain; the aptly-named length of Wenlock Edge with its steep western face and gently eastern slope bordering dreamy Corve Dale; the Clees, in parts rugged as many of their fellows over the border. But today there are probably none more popular with the rambling fraternity than the Stiperstones, a range of hills of Ordovician origin, running up to 1,731 feet at the highest point, and taking their name from the masses of outcropping igneous rock, traditionally an apronful spilt by Old Nick after he had built the "Devil's Chair" near the summit, and which give the range a peculiarly jagged mountain-like aspect when viewed in sunset silhouette; the hills present on the lower slopes hanging oak woods and on the bleak uplands heather and bracken silent but for the piping of the curlews and the ticking of the wheatears.

The beginnings of the mining industry of the Stiperstones are lost in the mists of antiquity, but it is known that lead was obtained from shallow borings in Roman times and traces of their old workings are still to be seen in the Hope district; a lead pig bearing the inscription of the Emperor Hadrian (A.D. 117—138), found at Snailbeach, is preserved in the British Museum. Throughout the succeeding centuries, mining continued in a haphazard manner, periods of activity alternating with periods of idleness, and the borings gradually going deeper as the older surface workings became exhausted; some mines are shown on a map of Shropshire dated 1705, and by the 19th century there were in existence a small number of moderately-sized mining concerns, while the country around was scarred with overgrown mounds of debris and enclosed shafts.

Full development of the mining resources was hampered by the lack of adequate transport facilities — the Stiperstones then, as now, was a rural solitude with poor roads, often little better than tracks, and the mines themselves were in general remote even from these; paths were beaten to the shaft heads, to fall into disuse when the workings were exhausted; in short, circumstances commonly fertile in the early development of the iron road. But local enterprise here was restricted to very short systems between mines and tip (as at The Bog) or to a nearby road, and the 19th century was more than half gone before rail connection of the valley with the outside world was established in the form of the joint G.W.-L.N.W. branch from Hanwood Junction to Minsterley, opened June 1st. 1861; though there had been earlier but fruitless schemes to run the whole length of the Rea valley.

The Minsterley branch was not, however, of much help to the various mining firms away out on the bleak hillside and as with the passage of the next decade there seemed little prospect of the main line companies taking any further interest in the area (it will be recalled that the ill-fated Potteries, Shrewsbury and North Wales Railway had already fallen on hard times because of the smallness of local traffic) a number of the leading mining concerns (in particular the Snailbeach Mine Co. Ltd.) and others locally interested conceived a plan to build an independent railway from the Stiperstones to Pontesbury, the penultimate station of the Minsterley branch. A narrow gauge was advocated in the interests of economy of materials, whilst cheapness in running would be assured by reason of the route being almost entirely downhill for the loaded wagons; surveying commenced at Minsterley on May 17th 1872 and plans were deposited at Shrewsbury on November 27th of that year.

The Snailbeach District Railways Company was incorporated by Act of Parliament (36 and 37 Vic Cap 207) dated August 5th, 1873, and was authorised to consist of two railways of 2ft. 4in. gauge, though it was stipulated that the earthworks should be made to accommodate standard gauge track. Railway No. 1 — 3 miles, 2 furlongs, 5.44 chains in length — was to run roughly south-south-east from a junction just west of Pontesbury station to Crowsnest, at the more distant end of Snailbeach village; Railway No. 2 was to be a continuation of this line along a shelf of the Stiperstones to one of the Earl of Tankerville's lead mines at Pennerley, in the same general direction, and 1 mile, 7 furlongs, 3.90 chains in length (see map). The Directors were Colonel Heaton Lovett, John Henkin Lovett, John Jones (Secretary), John Vincent Hawkesley Williams, Joseph Whitehouse and Theodore Martin, and the Engineer was Henry Dyke Dennis of Ruabon; in later years the railway was almost entirely in the hands of the Dennis family. John Jones was succeeded as Secretary by Henry Williams, who held the office until 1890. The firm of Longueville, Jones and Williams of Oswestry took care of legal affairs. The authorised capital was £20,000 in £10 shares (of which the Snailbeach Mine Co. were allowed to subscribe not more than £2,000) and the Company were empowered to raise a further £6,600 by loan or debenture.

The Company did not find it easy to obtain the capital required to commence operations, since they had to rely almost entirely on the mine owners for support, the railway being in a relatively remote district where alternative sources of revenue were then lacking, though this was not so in later years. It is also true that only a few of the lead mines would be directly served by the railway and some of the larger concerns, in particular the mine of the Stiperstones Mining Co. Ltd. at The Bog, were some miles away from the railhead, and so it is hardly to be wondered at that their contributions were not very liberal. Finally, it was not intended to cater for passengers, and the general public as a consequence took little interest in the venture. Up to the end of 1875 only £6,750 had been subscribed, but in the following year, due to extra efforts by the Snailbeach Mine Co., a further £8,970 ordinary share capital was paid up and £4,000 raised by loan; work was then actively pushed forward and Railway No. 1 was opened for traffic in July 1877.

LAYOUT AND EQUIPMENT

It will be convenient here to describe the route and equipment of the S.D.R., as the "Railway No. 1" of the 1873 Act was the only section ever actually constructed, and, apart from one or two sidings and a branch line to be described later, the layout remained essentially unaltered throughout the railway's existence. As already mentioned, the line was designed to run from a point on the Minsterley branch about a quarter of a mile west of Pontesbury station to Crowsnest, the direction being roughly south-south-east, though the course of the line was by no means straight. The gauge selected was 2ft. 4in., but has sometimes been referred to as 2ft. 3¾ in. The origin of this version is unknown to the writer, but Mr. W.H. Austen quoted it when writing to the Salop County Council on December 12th 1932; the 1873 Act gives the gauge as 2ft. 4in., and in the Special Return to the Board of Trade dated December 31st 1898 which specifically required railways to state their gauge, the S.D.R. gave theirs as 2ft. 4in. The narrow gauge necessitated the provision of transhipment sidings at Pontesbury Junction, where a standard gauge siding was put in, with points and associated disc signals controlled from a ground frame; and the layout was such that the aid of gravity was enlisted in transferring goods from narrow to standard gauge wagons and vice versa. One S.D.R. siding was carried on stout oak piers above the standard gauge metals, whilst another siding was run into a cutting alongside. As most of the S.D.R. wagons were of the hopper variety, transhipment from them was merely a matter of opening the trap-door in the body, but in the reverse direction shovelling was necessary.

In the vicinity of Pontesbury there were also a few other sidings for the reception of wagons, and near the end of these the rails crossed the Shrewsbury to Minsterley road by a girder bridge on stone abutments; beyond here the line became single and, plunging into a tree-lined cutting with a stream chuckling at the side, began immediately to climb; the gradient of 1 in 38.8 was maintained for just over two miles. About ¾ mile from Pontesbury the line passed under a wooden bridge carrying a farm track and soon emerged from the cutting to skirt Callow Hill, an isolated granite outcrop, the quarrying on which was later to provide the major traffic of the railway; at the time of opening, and for many years afterwards, the only quarry on the hill lay on the eastern side, remote from the railway, and its output was conveyed by road. Still climbing, the railway was carried on a shelf in the shade of the woods clinging to the hillside, crossed a rocky cascading stream 28 feet below, and then joined on the western side a narrow lane leading from Minsterley, which paralleled the line for a few hundred yards and was then embanked to cross it by a substantial stone skew bridge. A lineside smithy was built opposite to this lane, presumably for the convenience of maintenance men living at Minsterley, and repairs to rails, etc., were carried out here. As late as 1948 the blower and a motley collection of old rails, point levers, anti-trespass notices, etc., remained as evidence of former prosperity.

11

Exchange sidings at Pontesbury, with Minsterley branch in the background, about 1925.
(Courtesy Ian Allan Ltd.)

Locomotive No. 4 on the bridge over the main road at Pontesbury, December 19th, 1941.
(J.G. Vincent)

No. 3 shunting at Pontesbury on December 19th, 1941.　　　　　*(J.G. Vincent)*

Overbridge near Minsterley, October 11th, 1947.　　　　　*(J.L. Brown)*

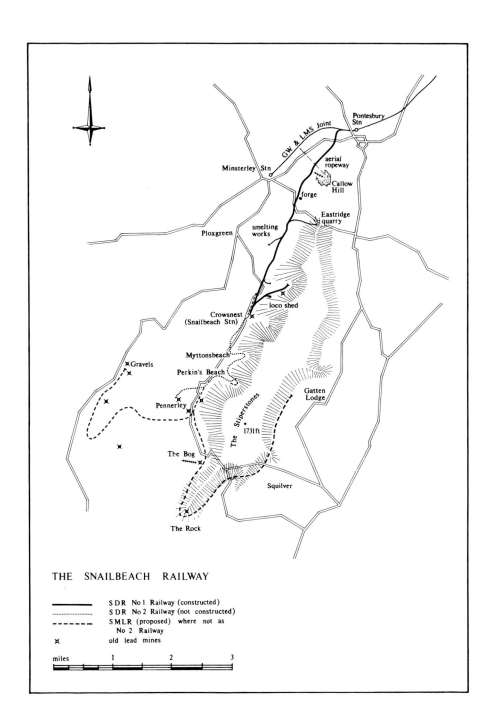

THE SNAILBEACH RAILWAY

⎯⎯⎯ S D R No 1 Railway (constructed)
.... S D R No 2 Railway (not constructed)
⎯ ⎯ ⎯ S M L R (proposed) where not as
              No 2 Railway
✕ old lead mines

miles   1   2   3

For the next half-mile the railway ran through shady over-hanging oak woods, a delight in spring and dankly warm in winter, and then emerged into more open country, the woods receding to the Stiperstones range, now appearing about a quarter-mile to the left. The gradient eased very slightly to 1 in 43.6, then 1 in 40, finishing with two chains at 1 in 84, and the line crossed two minor streams, respectively 26 and 15 feet below rails, in its curving ascent towards Snailbeach: 2¾ miles from Pontesbury the Minsterley-Pennerley road was carried over the railway by a stone bridge, only to double back a quarter-mile further on to re-cross the line by another bridge and run alongside it to the terminus at Crowsnest. The two bridges just mentioned were similar to the one near Minsterley, except that the Crowsnest bridge had iron railings instead of a stone parapet. For the last half-mile or so the railway was practically straight and at Crowsnest there was siding accommodation, a loading deck with crane supplied by Messrs. W.H. Hughes of Plaskynaston, Ruabon, and weighbridges for road and rail vehicles, collectively known as "Snailbeach Station".

So much for "Railway No. 1" of the S.D.R. Act, in addition to which two branches were constructed. One of these ran from a junction about a mile from Crowsnest, in a south-westerly direction to the smelting works, which dealt with lead ore from the various mines in the vicinity. The single line from the junction soon divided into two, one for ore running to the east side of the works (which were situated on a hillside) and the other, for the products of the works, to the rear or west side. Traces of this junction and the course of the line are still visible. The other branch made a trailing junction at Snailbeach station and ran for a quarter-mile at an incline of about 1 in 25, behind the houses of Snailbeach village and, overhung by woods most of the way, to the shafts of the Snailbeach Mine Co. The latter are dotted about the hillside, and the various buildings were connected by an extensive series of sidings. The principal buildings were situated on an artificial plateau which started out as the spoil-bank of earlier workings; and here, at the head of the incline, was located the two-road engine shed, a solidly constructed granite building with rather curious cowls for "pots", reminiscent of a church belfry. The shed was equipped with a lathe, smithy's furnace and other tackle for the carrying out of running repairs to locomotives and wagons, together with some rather primitive lifting equipment. In later years a spoil-bank siding was thrown across the approach to the shed and provided the classic spot for locomotive photographers. Snailbeach shed stood 600 feet above sea level, 45 feet directly above the main line to Pontesbury and 430 feet above the level of Pontesbury Junction; and from it a magnificent view across the Rea Valley is obtained, embracing Long Mountain overlooking Welshpool, the Breiddens and a score of minor tree-clad hills before Montgomery.

The lines described are those with which the S.D.R. commenced work and thus in essentials it remained. Subsequently minor changes occurred, but these only affected sidings and branches to works, the main line remaining unaltered. Railway No. 2 was never completed nor even any earthworks begun; the proposed route is shown on the map. This railway would have been more expensive than No. 1 as it was to be carried on a shelf of the hillside most of the way, and would have necessitated two high bridges over streams — one 65 feet high at Crowsnest Dingle and one of 46 feet at Perkins Beach; again, it was designed for a rising gradient throughout, 7½ furlongs at 1 in 36.17, followed by 6½ furlongs at 1 in 39, — and 1 furlong, 3.9 chains at 1 in 54.82, bringing the terminus to 729 feet above sea level.

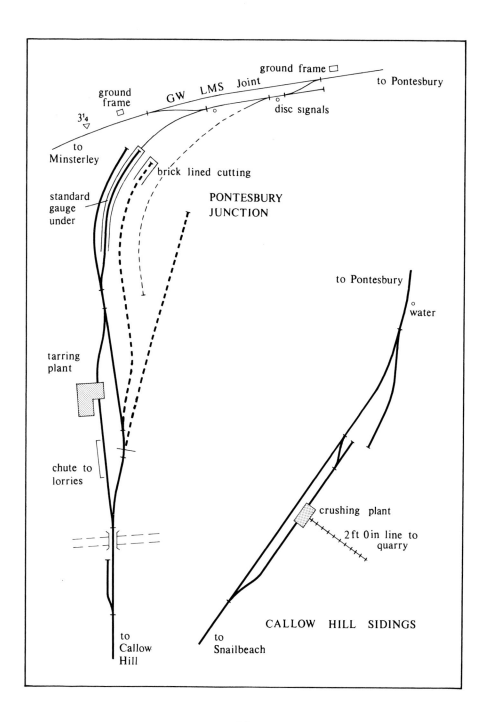

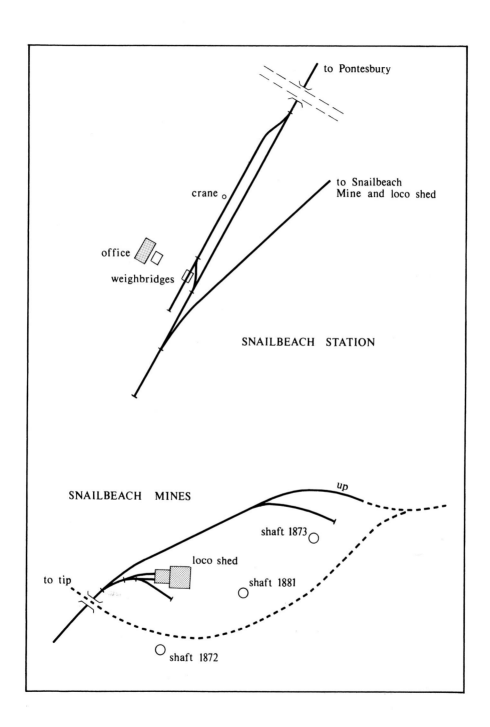

to Pontesbury

crane

to Snailbeach
Mine and loco shed

office

weighbridges

SNAILBEACH STATION

SNAILBEACH MINES

up

shaft 1873

loco shed

shaft 1881

to tip

shaft 1872

A view of the line near Eastridge Wood on May 26th, 1948.   *(E.S. Tonks)*

View along line, looking towards Snailbeach Station, and taken from Plox Green road
bridge.   *(Photomatic Ltd.)*

View from Snailbeach Station, showing the crane, on October 11th, 1947.   (J.L. Brown)

Snailbeach Station. Line to locomotive shed and mines to the right, office and weigh-house to left of van. October 11th, 1947.   (J.L. Brown)

The rails were of the spiked type, 40 lbs. per yard, and the sharpest curve 3½ chains radius. No signals were provided, the line being operated on the "one engine in steam" principle.

Snailbeach Locomotive Shed. Nos. 2, 4 and the remains of DENNIS. *Note the reversing line to the mines in background. Photographed about 1925.* *(courtesy Ian Allan Ltd.)*

HISTORY OF THE S.D.R.

1877 - 1914

As regards its early history, the S.D.R. can best be described in the words of a bygone Mayor of Shrewsbury as "a mutual benefit kind of railway". The line owed its promotion, and its existence for some thirty years, to the local lead mining industry, which in its turn benefited to a not inconsiderable extent by the cheaper transport provided by the railway, as evidenced by the number of shafts sunk in the 70's and 80's. When the railways opened in 1877, some £16,000 of the share capital had been subscribed, and the full amount of £20,000 was realised by 1884, together with £2,200 in loan and debenture stock, which figures remained stationary until 1900.

For the years 1878–1883 inclusive the average annual tonnage of minerals carried by the railway was 14,000 tons, plus a very small amount of parcels and other merchandise, representing about 1% of the total. This period of prosperity was reflected in the rising receipts of the railway company, who paid a 3% dividend on ordinary shares for each of the years 1877–9 and 1881–3, but the year 1884 brought a sharp reversal of fortune. The Tankerville Great Consols Co. (Tankerville Mining Co. Ltd. until January 1881) which operated mines at Tankerville, Pennerley and The Bog, and was one of the S.D.R.'s biggest customers, closed down in June 1884, and the annual tonnage on the S.D.R. fell to the 5500 mark. As a result, dividends ceased, the last payment being February 19th 1884.

As would be expected, the Snailbeach Mine Co. was the S.D.R.'s best customer, since the railway had direct access to the workings and were able to convey all the ore to the smelting works lower down the Hope Valley and thence to Pontesbury for handing over to the main line companies. In this connection it may be mentioned that the chairs of the standard gauge siding at Pontesbury were dated 1881, which suggests that Pontesbury Junction was not brought into use until the S.D.R. had been operating for some years. According to Mr. Hewitt, the smelting works was in operation before the S.D.R. was built, the ore being "trammed" to the works through the woods. The more remote lead mines were not very much better off for the advent of their narrow gauge railway, which did however benefit to some extent when these companies sent ore to the Snailbeach smelting works, and the S.D.R. conveyed the resulting metal the last 2½ miles to Pontesbury. An aerial ropeway (two piers remained for many years) was erected between the Gravels lead mines and the smelting works, but the products of other mines were conveyed by road to Snailbeach. The lack of this potential traffic, particularly that of the important mine at The Bog belonging to the Stiperstones Mining Co., was a source of much concern to the directorate of the S.D.R., and the dissatisfaction crystallised in the promulgation of a new but associated company to provide the rail facilities desired – The Shropshire Minerals Light Railway.

Plans were drawn up by the Engineers of the proposed railway, Geo. W. Usill, and deposited at Shrewsbury on November 29th, 1890, and no difficulty was experienced in raising the money to meet initial expenses, or in the form of objections to the scheme as a whole, which received the Royal assent on August 5th, 1891, eighteen years to the day after the S.D.R. was incorporated. The official title of the railway is interesting as being one of the first to include the word "Light"; before the passing of the Light Railways Act of 1896 the title "Light Railway" had not the special legal significance of implying simplicity of construction and operating methods. The inclusion in the present instance was probably due in some measure to a desire to avoid confusion with a scheme of half a century earlier for the Shropshire Minerals Railway, devised to serve the industrial area of Coalbrookdale.

The S.M.L.R. was from the start a much more ambitious scheme than the parent Snailbeach line, totalling more than 11 route miles of track and wending its circuitous way within siding distance of practically every lead mine in the district. It was naturally to be laid to the 2ft. 4in. gauge of the S.D.R., with which physical connection was to be made at the northern end of Snailbeach village. The proposed course of the line is shown on the map; for the first half-mile it parallels the S.D.R. to Crowsnest and then roughly follows the site of the unfulfilled "Railway No. 2" of the older company, calling for a 100-yard viaduct at Myttons Beach* and one of 93 yards at Perkins Beach*; but short of the original terminus the S.M.L.R. diverges southward and runs past The Bog mine to Rock House mine and, skirting Nipstone Rock, runs more or less northward again to the vicinity of Gatten Lodge on the north-east side of the Stiperstones. The object of this lengthy projection was presumably to tap the barytes mines in this district, which were then beginning to oust lead as the principal mineral wealth of the neighbourhood. A branch line was also contemplated, from Pennerley to Roman Gravels lead mines. The S.M.L.R. was divided into three railways for parliamentary purposes: No. 1, from Snailbeach to Rock House mine (2miles, 4 furlongs, 4 chains); No. 2 – the branch – 4 miles, 4 furlongs, 3 chains; and No. 3, from Rock House mine to Gatten Lodge (4 miles, 2 furlongs, 8 chains).

As a glance at a contoured map will show, this railway would have been an expensive one to build and to operate, for much of the rail-bed would have to be blasted out of rocky hillside, and it was a proper switchback throughout, abounding in banks of 1 in 30(both up and down) and with but a few hundred yards of level track in the whole of its tortuous length. It is, then, perhaps hardly surprising that the requisite capital was not forthcoming, especially considering the hard job the S.D.R. had to raise the money required for their mere 3½ miles of track. But a more cogent reason lay behind the tardiness of the mine owners in supporting this grandiose venture; the lead mining industry of the Stiperstones was decaying, the heavy expenses incurred by deeper boring making the price of the ore uneconomic. The

* The word "Beach" occurs in the names of several places in this vicinity and bears the same significance as in Wisbech, implying a watercourse.

smelting works had closed and the small amount of lead ore still mined was sent away in the raw state for processing. One by one the mines were perforce closing and the S.M.L.R. as a result never progressed beyond the paper stage; had it done so, the combined undertaking would have been one of the longest narrow gauge mineral systems in England.

The mild flutter caused by the promotion of the S.M.L.R. soon died down and the railway relegated to Limbo; meanwhile the S.D.R. kept plugging along, just about managing to keep its head above water up to 1898, but afterwards declining and showing operating losses for most years in the next decade; though the actual tonnage carried did not vary very much. At the turn of the century, however, it was clear that the lead mining industry of the Stiperstones was doomed to extinction ere long and the future of the S.D.R. looked black indeed, when rescue came, sensational in its small way. The Ceiriog Granite Co. opened a quarry on the north side of Eastridge wood, near Habberley, and a branch line to this quarry was constructed, leaving the S.D.R. about two miles from Pontesbury. The Chairman of the S.D.R., Sir Henry Dyke Dennis, was on the board of the Glyn Valley Tramway Co., which latter line served the principal quarries of the Ceiriog Granite Company, and it is likely that he used his influence with the quarry company in order to save the S.D.R. from extinction. In anticipation of a substantial increase in receipts from the stone traffic, the railway raised £4,100 by 4% debenture, bringing the total of such stock to £6,300, to meet the expenses of this branch and catch up on the arrears of repairs caused by the slump in the lead traffic.

The branch was opened for traffic in 1905 and resulted in the following year in the conveyance of over 20,000 tons of mineral traffic for the first time in the railway's history; this happy state of affairs continued for five years, the best year being 1909, when over 38,000 tons of goods were carried, and then trade fell off once more, with the debenture interest in arrear.

HISTORY OF THE S.D.R.

1914 ~ 1946

The fortunes of the S.D.R. continued in this downward trend; the Snailbeach mine of the Snailbeach Lead Mining Co. (Snailbeach Mine Co. Ltd. until August 1885) had closed and the siding to the smelting works taken up. There remained the dwindling stone traffic from the Eastridge branch, plus a small amount from felspar quarried at Snailbeach (lower level), for which a short siding was laid; some coal was also conveyed up the valley and occasional loads of timber went down to Pontesbury. The war of 1914–1918 intensified the financial difficulties, the stone traffic ceasing altogether, and rendering the railway unable to meet its now increased liabilities; by 1920 the traffic was very small and intermittent, and the Board consequently only too glad to transfer their responsibilities to someone with sufficient enthusiasm to see hope for the line. Such a man was Colonel Stephens, the first and foremost advocate of the minor railway, and his colleagues on the new board were Messrs. H.M. Bates, J.C. White and Sir R.F. Bowmaker; the retiring board consisted of Sir Henry Dyke Dennis (Chairman), W.P. Dennis, W. Edmunds, M.D. Lawford; Arthur H. Bardwell was the late Secretary, a position he had held for more than thirty years; the old offices were located in Oswestry, but were now transferred to Tonbridge, Kent.

The new management took office from January 1st, 1923 (an incident forgotten in the concurrent amalgamation upheaval of the main line companies), inheriting an accumulated debt of £4,531, and immediately set about the task of putting the railway into good working order. The permanent way was cleaned up, most of the sleepers being replaced by halves of secondhand standard sleepers, and the track from Pontesbury to the felspar siding relaid with heavier rails, weighing 45 lbs. to the yard; the disused Eastridge branch was taken up in 1922, and its course is now an impenetrable thicket, and the quarry water-logged, though traces of the junction are still to be seen. Three locomotives were purchased to assist the solitary survivor from the Dennis era, and some thirty odd wagons purchased secondhand from the Government. Finally, land was purchased to enable the line to reach Pontesbury station, with the rather ambitious object of catering for passengers; it is hardly necessary to add that this project was never carried out.

The improved efficiency of the line encouraged traffic, which steadily grew, the annual tonnage passing the 10,000 mark in 1929 and reaching 26,352 in 1938. The lead traffic had vanished with the closure of the last lead mine in 1911; the Black Tom barytes mine was opened about 1922, and a new source of revenue appeared in the opening up of a new quarry on Callow Hill by Haywards' Quarries Ltd.; a 2ft. 0in. gauge system operated in the quarry itself, the wagon loads of granite being

Notice on the Minsterley-Habberley road bridge. This appears to be a standard County Council notice with their title replaced by "Snailbeach & Dst Railways" in different lettering. The "locomotives" referred to are road locomotives. *(Photomatic Ltd.)*

No. 3 shunting at Callow Hill on December 19th, 1941. *(J.G. Vincent)*

pushed by hand to the crushing plant under which ran a S.D.R. siding, so that granite chippings could be loaded directly into railway wagons beneath. A few years later, the Shropshire County Council leased the quarry from the owners and erected a tarring plant alongside the S.D.R. at Pontesbury, close to the road bridge. Hopper wagons from the quarry discharged their contents as required either directly into lorries below or down a chute into the plant for tarring and subsequent removal by lorries for road-mending purposes. Stretching over the railway and beyond the summit of the hill was an aerial ropeway of the Malehurst Barytes Co., running down to the G.W.R. Minsterley line, but this had ceased to operate probably around the time the Callow Hill quarry was opened.

Colonel Stephens died in 1931 and was succeeded for a short period by a Mr. Ramsey (formerly rolling stock controller on the Caledonian Railway) and then by Mr. W.H. Austen as Director and Engineer. By 1932 the railway was dependant entirely on the Callow Hill quarry for traffic, and the transfer siding at Pontesbury fell into disuse; the annual tonnage carried was still increasing, producing a small profit, but not enough to pay interest on ordinary shares, and maintenance expenses were kept to a minimum. The method of working was a little odd; the loaded wagons were allowed to run down to Pontesbury by gravity, a few at a time, with a braked van in train; the locomotive was steamed on Mondays, Wednesdays and Fridays and its sole task consisted in hauling the accumulated empties back to Callow Hill, a mile trip involving six times the distance of light mileage to and from Snailbeach shed, which must have offset the saving due to the help of gravity.

During the twenties the staff consisted of one driver-cum-fitter named Gatford, who had served earlier on the Bishops Castle Railway, and a platelayer who occasionally helped him, but, from the middle thirties, Driver Gatford ran the railway single-handed — a unique achievement. He kept the engines in running order very well, considering the limited resources at his disposal; also the wagons, of which there were a number considerably in excess of everyday requirements. The permanent way was rather beyond his powers, however, and apart from providing occasional fresh sleepers he did not give it much attention, with the result that the track of the Pontesbury-Callow Hill section became rather worn and out of alignment; other parts became weedy, but as the line was used as a public footpath by villagers and quarrymen it did not become too overgrown.

The little windswept stone shed held only two engines and when the locomotive stock was increased to four, a peculiarly barn-like extension was built, in the form of a corrugated iron roof on wooden pillars, in front of the shed doors; the sheets rusted away and the wind in the hills tore them down, but the pillars remained to the everlasting annoyance of photographers. After the demise of *Dennis,* there was still one engine unsheltered, and this was left at any convenient spot — in the open by the felspar siding, or under the road bridge, as the driver chose; his cottage backed on to the railway just below the shed and latterly, when he was over 70, he used to leave the engine (after taking on coal and water) outside his garden gate, ready for the next day's work. The driver was a conscientious man and there was more than enough to keep him busy; stores he used to obtain from Kinnerley S. and M. shed, who also sent him help for any heavy task, but he was not very well provided with

A derailment of one of the hopper wagons at Callow Hill on December 19th, 1941.
(J.G. Vincent)

Loaded wagons descending by gravity from Callow Hill on December 19th, 1941.
(J.G. Vincent)

tools. Even in the 1939–45 war he managed to obtain a little red and white paint and brightened up the engine buffer beams, with the addition of the numbers in bold letters and figures.

With the S.D.R. catering solely for the quarry traffic the Salop County Council considered taking over the line and on December 6th 1932 Mr. W.H. Austen sent the following particulars of the railway (which differs in some details from the foregoing).

Finance	Ordinary share capital — £20,000 in £10 shares; Debentures £6,300 at 4½%.
Physical data.	Gauge — 2ft. 3¾in, length — 3 miles 31 chains excluding sidings.
Rolling Stock.	4 locos (including one dismantled) and 42 wagons.
Staff.	One driver-fitter; one platelayer; one junctionman and brakeman.

Finally Mr. Austen stated that the Executors of the late Colonel Stephens would be prepared to accept £4,250 for the railway. The County Council, however, decided not to take up the offer and wrote to this effect January 21st 1933. The reason was that they would require Parliamentary sanction to do so, and their lease of the quarry was for a limited peroid only; an alternative put forward but not acted upon was that the quarry owners should acquire the line themselves. The S.D.R. therefore carried on as before, but eventually was leased to the S.C.C. fourteen years later.

LOCOMOTIVES

AND ROLLING STOCK

The first locomotive was obtained in 1877 and was an 0-4-2ST named *Belmont*: she was apparently obtained from Henry Hughes of Loughborough, and the book of accounts contains several references to payments to this firm presumably for spares. She worked the traffic unaided until 1881 when the Statement of Accounts of August 23rd 1881 reports a "new engine received, working and paid for". The suppliers were Lennox Lange of Glasgow, though it is unlikely that this firm were the builders; it has been suggested she may have been built by Barclays & Co. This loco was an 0-6-0ST named *Fernhill* and it would seem that it took over the bulk of the work for the next six years, as no more spares were ordered for *Belmont* until 1887 (from the Falcon Engine & Car Works, as Henry Hughes had become by then); it was then *Belmont's* turn to do the major share of the work. Very little else is known of these engines, neither of which survived to Colonel Stephens' time. There was a 2ft. 6in. gauge 0-6-0ST named *Fernhill* built by Stephen Lewin in 1875 and offered for sale in Waterford in 1879 by the Bonmahon Copper Mining Co., and on the basis of the common name it has been suggested that she became the S.D.R. loco. However the fact that *Belmont* and *Fernhill* were respectively the names of the residences of Col. Heaton Lovett and John Henkin Lovett (both S.D.R. Directors at the time) strongly suggests that the names were the original S.D.R. locos and the identification of one with the Lewin not so likely after all. The ultimate fate of these two engines is not known with certainty, but one is believed to have been scrapped about 1906 (when a further engine arrived) and the other during World War 1.

The opening of the Eastridge branch called for extra power and the Glyn Valley Tramway Co. lent them *Sir Theodore,* a 0-6-0T built by Beyer Peacock, for trials; it will be recalled that the presence at that time of Sir Henry Dyke Dennis on the boards of both concerns enabled some pooling of ideas and resources. Unfortunately, the gauge of the G.V.T. being 2ft. 4½in., the flanges of *Sir Theodore* kept riding up the sides of the S.D.R. metals, and the engine was soon returned to its original owners; in its place a new engine was ordered in December 1905 from Messrs. W.G. Bagnall Ltd., of Stafford. It was delivered to Pontesbury in February 1906, a six coupled side tank named *Dennis,* works number 1797, which had 12in. x 18in. cylinders, 2ft. 9¼in. driving wheels, 150 lbs.sq.in. working pressure and a weight of 20 tons in working order. Bagnall — Price valve gear was fitted and the locomotive had cost £970. The frames were outside the wheels. Brass nameplates were carried on the tank sides and the loco was painted in standard Bagnall livery — green with red and yellow lining. This engine was the only one surviving in 1922 when Colonel Stephens took over the railway, but even then was in poor condition, having had very little attention since its arrival; Colonel Stephens therefore took immediate steps to

DENNIS – *the photograph taken by the makers when she was built.*   *(W.G. Bagnall Ltd.)*

increase the stock and *Dennis*, which was then given the number 1, was laid by for a thorough overhaul. It was destined, however, never to run again; Driver-Fitter Gatford seems to have taken a dislike to the engine and, in the course of some occasionally caustic correspondence with his chief, put forward a number of reasons why the repairs to *Dennis* were delayed, e.g., it was impossible to remove the firebox without removing the back plate of the boiler, etc. The makers were approached and they showed how the work could be done; but driver Gatford had the last word and *Dennis* remained in bits outside Snailbeach shed. Officially withdrawn from service in 1936, by the autumn of 1937 only the wheels, frame, cylinders and boiler casing remained; by January, 1938, only the wheels; one nameplate survived many years amongst the ashes of the forge.

Colonel Stephens purchased three engines, as mentioned earlier. The first of these was an 0-4-2T built in 1902 by Kerr Stuart & Co Ltd, of Stoke on Trent. It had 7½in. x 12in. cylinders, driving wheels 2ft. 3in., trailing wheels 1ft. 1in., working pressure 160 lbs., and a weight in working order of 9 tons 15 cwt. The early history is unknown but it was at the Admiralty's Ridham General Salvage Depot at Sittingbourne, Kent, during the First World War; by September 1920 the locomotive, then named *Skylark*, seems to have been at the Central Stores Depot, Neasden, London, from where it was being advertised "in good condition" by the Ministry of Munitions Disposals Board. The S.D.R. acquired the engine, which became their No. 2, via dealer E.C. Cornforth of Stoke on Trent in 1922. It was originally of 2ft. 6in. gauge, but was easily converted – possibly by Cornforth – for use on the S.D.R.; it had outside framing and an inspection slot in the side tank, making it very similar to *Dennis*, but was painted plain black.

30

The other side of No. 2; the brake gear was disconnected when the photograph was taken.
(Courtesy Ian Allan Ltd.)

No. 2 at Snailbeach shed on June 11th, 1943.   *(L.W. Perkins)*

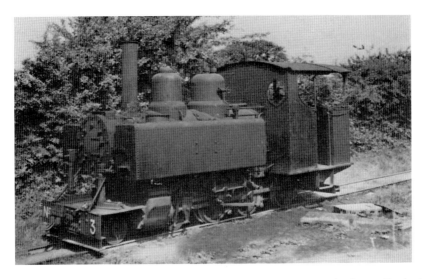

No. 3 at Callow Hill — compare with No. 4 for detail differences.   *(authors collection)*

No. 4 at Callow Hill on May 5th, 1940 with Driver Gatford in charge. Note the "blinkers"
to the cab windows and the water-lifting divice to the side tank.   *(J.G. Vincent)*

Locomotives Nos. 3 and 4 were two 4-6-0 side tanks of the class built in considerable numbers by the Baldwin Locomotive Company of America for use on the 60 cm. gauge lines laid in France during World War 1, their principal dimensions being: 9in. x 12in. cylinders; 1ft. 11½in. driving wheels; 1ft. 4in. bogie wheels; 178 lbs.sq.in. working pressure; 14 tons 10cwt. weight in working order. These engines were of typical American outline and their rugged construction – to enable them to be used on hastily-laid and uneven track – made them suitable for narrow gauge railway operation where smooth running was not the primary requisite. Many of them were pretty badly knocked about during their war service, including the present two, which were rebuilt by Messrs. Bagnalls in 1918; their W.D. nos. were 538 and 722, respectively Baldwin's nos. 44383 of 1916 and 44572 of 1917, and they carried their W.D. number plates on the side tanks when they commenced work on the S.D.R. in January, 1923; they were removed later. S.D.R. numbers were painted on the buffer beams in white, the rest of the livery being plain black. The two engines were practically identical, but No. 4 was fitted with a water lifter on the left-hand side so that the tanks could be filled from streams, and the spectacles had "blinkers".

The three last-mentioned locos. worked all the traffic from 1923 up to the end of steam working in 1946. The railway company had very little to spare for repairs and maintenance, either in cash or staff, and Col. Stephens issued instructions that all three engines were to be used in turn for spells of 2–3 weeks; by this means, all were kept in reasonable running trim, and the excellence of this advice is reflected

This photograph of No. 4 in the 1920's shows items removed in later years – the chimney cover and the WD number plate for example. Note also the hose pipe bracket on the rear of the bunker and what could be evidence of a Bagnall works plate on the cab sheet.

(Courtesy Ian Allan Ltd.)

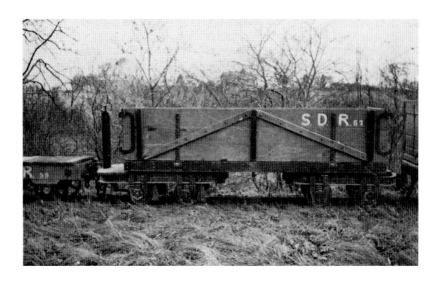

Bogie brake wagon at Pontesbury Sidings, December 19th, 1941. (J.G. Vincent)

in the fact that it was still being observed fifteen years after the Colonel's death. There was a sting in the tail, however; for all three became unserviceable about the same time, being condemned by the boiler inspector pending complete retubing.

When the railway commenced operations in 1877, the wagon stock was returned as 29 coal wagons, 12 hoppers, 6 timber wagons and 6 goods wagons – a total of 53. This figure was maintained until 1890 but in 1893 (the last available record) 52 is quoted, without breakdown into types. Very little is known about the design of these wagons, but they would appear to have been generally similar to the later ones; some were side-tippers, however. During the 1914–1918 war, however, many were disposed of and by 1921 only ten were left in running order. The stock was restored to its former strength by Colonel Stephens, who purchased a number of ex-Government narrow gauge vehicles for conversion to the 2ft. 4in. gauge, and all wagons were then numbered in 1–59, some of the older ones being renumbered in the process. Nos. 1–36 were hopper wagons with double buffers, of which 1–5,7,11, 12, and 16 were small capacity and 21 had a steel body, the rest having wood bodies. Nos. 37–50 were straight-sided coal wagons, of these, 39 and 42 had hand brakes and were supplied by Messrs. Bagnalls, 51–5/9 were flat wagons for lumber, but 51 later ran with a large "Royal Daylight" oil tank wired into position, for conveying oil to the screening plant. 56/7 were bogie straight-sided wagons, each with screw handbrakes fitted to one end, and with helical springs and central buffing and drawgear. 58 was a covered steel van with doors one side only, presumably for the conveyance of explosives to the quarry. All were painted grey, lettered S.D.R. in

Wagons for transporting coal, etc., at Pontesbury Sidings on December 19th, 1941.
(J.G. Vincent)

white, but 56/7 were originally red and beneath the paint on some could be read the lettering S.N.G.R. (presumably Snailbeach Narrow Gauge Railway) with the old number, e.g. 11,39,42,47 (originally 11,22,20,24). In 1949 all were to be seen except No. 40, whilst 22/6/7, and 31 were wrecked — having fallen off the pier at Pontesbury, but the only wagons in regular use were 17/8, 21/3/4/9, 30/1/4/6, 51, the rest all being stored in the sidings at Pontesbury and some at Callow Hill. There were also a few unidentifiable frames. The general design of the wagons was neat and their condition good.

THE LAST YEARS

As already mentioned, all three locomotives were withdrawn from service in in the summer of 1946, the last one in steam being No. 3, which ceased work in July. The dilemma caused by the wholesale immobilisation of motive power was overcome in a novel way, a Fordson tractor being hired to haul the empties from Pontesbury to Callow Hill. The "gauge" of the tractor, whose registration was BUX 174, was of course, about 5ft., so it ran with two wheels between the rails and two outside, the 1873 Act's insistence on the provision for standard gauge track alone making this possible. The output of the quarry remained at the same level, i.e., about 400 tons a week, but the tractor worked each day, including Saturdays, as required. For a time, Driver Gatford continued in charge of the "Loco.", but soon afterwards retired to his cottage at Snailbeach, to watch the weeds creeping over the metals beyond the hedge.

The tractor used for haulage when Salop C.C. took over the line. September 24th, 1947.
(H. Gray)

From April 14th, 1947, the Pontesbury — Callow Hill section was leased to the Shropshire County Council and from this date onwards the S.D.R. Company as such ceased to operate any service. The S.C.C. carried on as usual with the tractor, which at weekends was sheeted over near the crushing plant; about the same time, the tarring plant was dismantled and a new one erected at the top end of Pontesbury village, lorries conveying thither from the railway the grit for tarring, and wagons discharging on the south side of the road bridge. The grit had to be kept dry and in wet weather the wagons were sheeted over.

When the first edition of this book was written in 1950 the Snailbeach line was, of course, still active although parts of it largely disused. The following description of the railway as it existed at the time is perhaps worthy of repetition as a picture of a semi abandoned railway in an attractive if melancholy state. Then, "the enthusiast appreciative of the atmosphere peculiar to narrow gauge railways would do best to start from Pontesbury and walk the line to Snailbeach; this is, of course, technically trespass, but the well-worn path beside the rusting metals will allay his fears, indeed, some old warning notices (lettered S.D.R. or G.W.R.) of the type erected on road overbridges have been laid where ditches run athwart the path! As far as Callow Hill, the railway presents a workaday appearance, with muddy path and dusty hedges, though links with the past are provided by the pipeline still protruding from the ground near the quarry and formerly used for filling the tanks of the engines, and the long-disused aerial ropeway of the Malehurst Barytes Company, stretching over the railway and beyond the summit of the hill. The clangour of the crushing plant

Pontesbury Sidings, before the lorry transhipment siding was put in.
(R. W. Croughton: Real Photographs Co.Ltd.)

37

Pontesbury Sidings, looking towards the main-line sidings (hidden among trees). The shelter is adjacent to the tarring plant. September 24th, 1947. *(authors collection)*

Pontesbury Sidings, showing transhipment chute to S.C.C. lorries on October 11th, 1947. (J.L. Brown)

Pontesbury transhipment sidings in later days — there was not much weed clearance!
September 24th, 1947.   *(authors collection)*

After the end of steam haulage; the closed shed amid the ruins at Snailbeach on
October 11th, 1947. Compare the shed building with the photograph taken about 1925 — the
addition of smoke cowls and the ruinous extension.   *(J.L. Brown)*

recedes as we round the hill, past banks covered with foxgloves, and enter the green stillness of the woods. We can peer into the rubbish of the ruined forge here, and stumble along the grassy track under its canopy of trees to the neat bridge under the Minsterley lane, magpies and jays clamouring disapproval with our entry into their domain. The railway and its setting inevitably bring to mind some of the Welsh narrow gauge systems, more than any other the Talyllyn, with its climb up the hillside through the woods at Dolgoch. The dark brown rails make a nostalgic appeal to the imagination, as they always do, but it is difficult to say where the spirit of the railway abides most strongly — in the woods perhaps, or at Snailbeach where it was born.

"The track leading from Snailbeach station is now overgrown and in parts obliterated, and at the top of the slope passes under a frail bridge to the stone engine shed. Loco. No. 3 stands outside, cold and rusty but covered with a tarpaulin, and Nos. 2 and 4 behind the much-patched doors. The shed is an eerie and desolate place

Very shortly before they were cut up No. 2 and No. 3 bask in the sunshine at Snailbeach loco shed, April 21st, 1950. (G.F. Bannister; Gregory, Wolverhampton)

in winter, with the wind moaning in the cowls and banging the loose patches of corrugated iron, and how sad it is to look upon the forsaken and silent engines! No more will they snortingly push their trains up the bank to the mines or even clank their way down the curves to Pontesbury; instead, here they are, stranded among the rusty tools — the cobwebbed blower of the furnace and the old-fashioned well-worn lathe, its belting already rotting away — awaiting the end".

The railway did continue working, however, and the County Council operated the line for nearly ten years more. The traffic was as heavy as ever, but there was little glamour in the prosaic tractor, and the withdrawal of steam working took the colour from the railway. The locos and stock at Snailbeach were cut up on site by Thos. W. Ward Ltd. in May 1950 and the track between Snailbeach and Callow Hill removed shortly afterwards, but the track beyond the bridge by the loco shed was left intact and in the loco shed itself Richard Bowen noted a tractor in 1960. A number of changes were made; the 2ft. line in the quarry at Callow Hill was lifted and the work done by a dumper, and the wooden bridge three quarters of a mile from Pontesbury was replaced by a new structure of concrete, girder and stone for the use of lorries entering the quarry. On a visit in 1954, Vic Bradley found that all the coal and bogie wagons had gone, the rolling stock consisting of 24 hoppers (1,4,5,9,10, 13–6, 20/2/3/5/8,30–5 and four more) flat wagon 54 and the tank wagon on a disconnected piece of track. It will be noted that most of the wagons in use at the end of steam working had gone, replaced by others.

With lorries able to enter the quarry, the line was not likely to remain in use much longer, and tractor haulage ceased about the end of 1959, when the wagons in regular use until then were scrapped. The rest of the equipment was purchased by a local scrap dealer, Alfred Smith of Pontesford in 1961 and passed by him to the Wellington Coal & Iron Co. Ltd., who proceeded to dismantle the track from Callow Hill towards Pontesbury just before Christmas of that year. Some of the rail went to the Talyllyn Railway. In February 1962 the only track remaining was on the tipping dock by the road at Pontesbury; there were fifteen wagons awaiting scrap, including 5,13/4/6/7,20/4,33—the rest unidentifiable, having long been derelict here. Later in the year these trifling remains disappeared also; regrettably, none of the interesting hopper wagons were saved for preservation, though there had been hopes of one going to the Narrow Gauge Museum at Towyn. A frame, without wheels or body, lies behind a small brick shed at Kinnerley Junction (Shropshire & Montgomeryshire Rly), presumably brought there by a member of the Welsh Highland Light Railway Society, and a body lies upside down at Pontesbury Sidings. The only memento the author possesses is a nameplate of *Dennis*, but there are other small relics in the possession of local enthusiasts.

THE SNAILBEACH REMAINS

IN 1973

In one guise or another the Snailbeach line is still traceable and walkable for almost its entire length, and there are plenty of reminders of the more permanent features. The tipping area at Pontesbury is very heavily overgrown but the stone walls and stout timbers that supported the narrow gauge rails remain, and so do the tipping chutes to the County Council yard. The B.R. line to Minsterley was being lifted in January 1973 but the standard gauge siding in the S.D.R. exchange area is still there and seems likely to remain so; there is also a stub of narrow gauge track and the upturned and very ruinous body of one of the hopper wagons.

The bridge over the main road has been removed but the embankment remains and the formation to Callow Hill has been metalled to accommodate lorries, but is still a lovely wooded glade all the way. The route from Callow Hill to the Minsterley-Habberley lane is also given over to road transport but here the road formation is wider and the railway antecedents not obvious. The bridge under the lane has completely disappeared under a mound of rubble but immediately beyond the course of the line is clear all the way to Snailbeach; indeed, it is used as a public footpath as far as the narrow track a couple of hundred yards short of the Plox Green—Snailbeach road. Whether the route has official recognition as a footpath is not clear but it has certainly passed the statutory twenty years of unchallenged usage! Traces of the Eastridge Wood branch are to be seen near the junction, but the former route to the smelting works seems to have vanished without trace.

The section from the Plox Green—Snailbeach road to Crowsnest is extant but not readily passable, and the two bridges have been filled in. Adjacent to the Snailbeach road is the accumulation of felspar and other waste from the mines and this is now leased to a Mr. Joseph Roberts for making decorative garden slabs etc; in his yard are a couple of wooden mines tubs of 21in. gauge. The reversing section from Crowsnest to the loco. shed is still intact on its hillside shelf and the track is in position from the summit to the loco shed and beyond in two branches. It is not known why this section of track was not lifted with the rest, but the local theory is that it belonged to the mining companies and not to the S.D.R. Anyway, remain it does and so too the gem of an engine shed; not in very good condition but forthrightly proclaiming its identity to all. Long may it do so and encourage enthusiasts to make the delightful panoramic walk up from Pontesbury; the desolate mine shafts at Snailbeach are not beautiful — but the railway remains are.

Snailbeach "Station" office in August, 1972.   *(E.C. Griffith)*

The terminus at Crowsnest in August 1972. The railway was on the shelf at left.
(E.C. Griffith)

Engine shed at Snailbeach, August, 1972.   *(E.C. Griffith)*

Snailbeach. Bridge over track near the locomotive shed in August, 1972.   *(E.C. Griffith)*

Track and bridge near engine shed at Snailbeach (looking towards Crowsnest). August 1972　　　*(E.C. Griffith)*

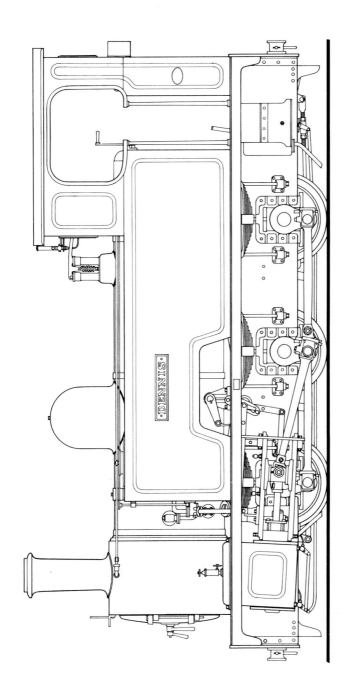

W. G. Bagnall   1797 of 1906   DENNIS

The Snailbeach District Railways

feet 0   2   4   6

Cylinders	12in x 18in
Coupled wheels	2ft 9¼in
Wheelbase (front)	4ft 3in
Wheelbase (rear)	4ft 3in
Length (over buffer beam)	19ft 1¾in
Overall height	10ft 10in
Overall width	7ft 6in
Heating surface (tubes)	380.2 sq ft
Heating surface (firebox)	49.2 sq ft
Heating surface (total)	429.4 sq ft
Grate area	6.5 sq ft
Copper firebox, brass tubes	
Working pressure	150 lbs sq in
Tractive effort (75%)	8750 lbs
Tank capacity	500 galls
Bunker capacity	20 cu ft
Weight in working order	20 tons
Boiler feed 2 no. 6mm injectors (Gresham's No 6)	
Fitted with steam brake	

These drawings, by Roger West, have been prepared from a copy of Bagnall drawing 6534, dated 5th February 1906, and kindly made available by Allan Baker and Allen Civil. The original is a pipe arrangement and appears to be the sole surviving contemporary drawing showing DENNIS. Details of the side rods, valve gear, axleboxes, etc. have had to be taken from the Bagnall official photograph, and the couplings from photographs of the locomotive when dismantled in the 1920's. The couplings do not appear on the drawing and are not visible on the works photograph; they may have been salvaged by the S.D.R. from the earlier locos, and fitted at Snailbeach. The Bagnall drawing is signed by W.S. Edwards, the Chief Draughtsman and later Managing Director, who had joined the firm from Kerr Stuart in 1901. Although the drawing clearly states the gauge as 2ft 4in, Bagnall's engine register gives the gauge as 2ft 3¾in.

47

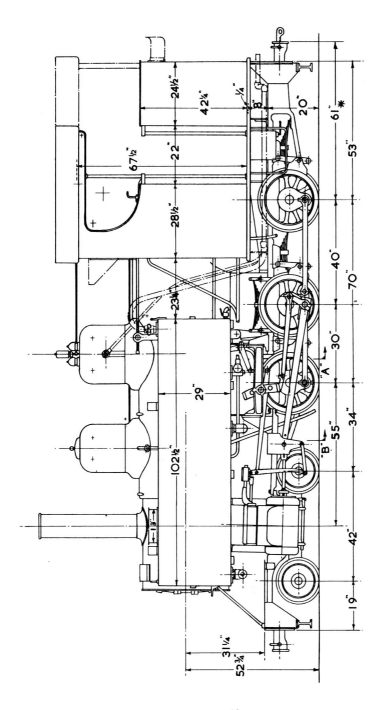

Baldwin Locomotive Co   4-6-0 side tanks

The Snailbeach District Railways

© D. Clayton 1957.

feet 0   2   4   6

48

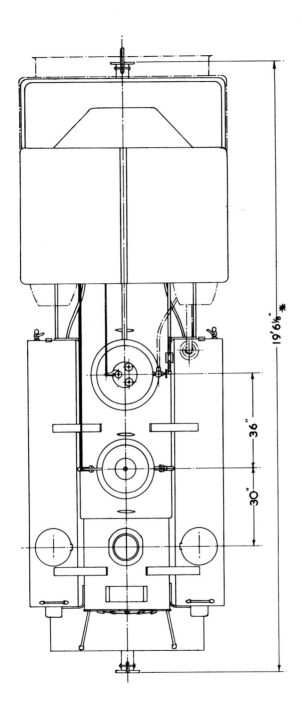

These drawings by Douglas Clayton, have been mainly prepared from data obtained from No. 3 in August 1946, with minor references to the Ashover Light Railway examples. The gauge shown on the drawings is the original 60 cm., the dimension required at Snailbeach being obtained by pulling out the tyres on the wheels. Photographs were used to obtain the shape of the smaller items such as pipes, brackets, etc. The pipes to and from the injector passing under the tank have been interrupted in order to show the hand brake and reversing lever bracket more clearly. The dimensions marked * are taken from a small W.D. diagram.

Items shown in broken line refer as follows. The cab extension was fitted to both No. 3 and No. 4 (probably by W.G. Bagnall). The steam pipe from the dome to below the cab and water pipe from the tank top to the rear of the cab are part of the water lifting equipment fitted only to No. 4 (as is the hose pipe carried on the rear of the bunker). The shields over the cab windows apply to No. 4 only.

49

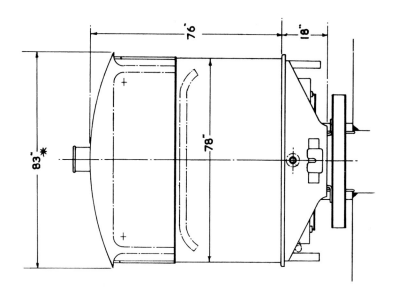

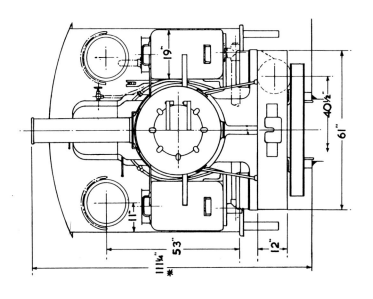

50

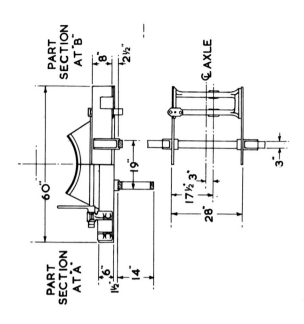

PART SECTION AT "B"

PART SECTION AT "A"

℄ AXLE

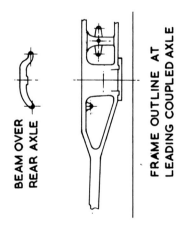

BEAM OVER REAR AXLE

FRAME OUTLINE AT LEADING COUPLED AXLE

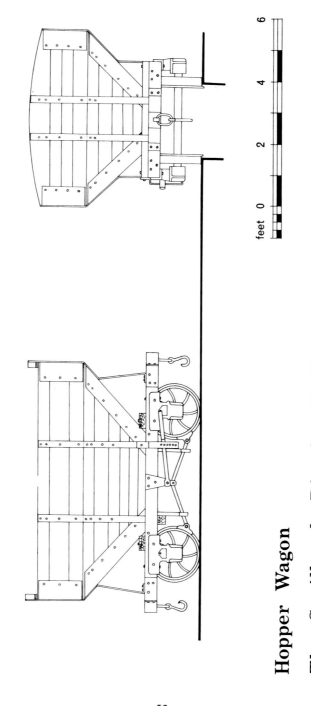

feet 0 2 4 6

Hopper Wagon

The Snailbeach District Railways

The drawing of the hopper wagon is by Philip Hindley from measurements taken at Pontesbury about 1960. The principal dimensions were: wheels 1ft. 7in. diameter; wheelbase 4ft. 7in.; length over body 7ft. 6in.; length overall 8ft. 3in.; width over body 5ft. 7in.; width over frames 3ft. 8¾in.; height overall 5ft. 7in. Timber body, sheet steel lined.